God's M

CW00504500

FINDING
**LIFE AND
HEALTH**
THROUGH GOD'S
WORD

GOD'S
MEDICINE
BOTTLE

DEREK PRINCE

ISBN 978-1-78263-566-6
Kindle 978-1-78263-568-0
ePub 978-1-78263-567-3
PRODUCT CODE T9

Derek Prince Ministries · www.derekprince.com

Set in Arno by Raphael Freeman, Renana Typesetting

Contents

My son, give attention to my words;
Incline your ear to my sayings.
Do not let them depart from your eyes;
Keep them in the midst of your heart;
For they are life to those who find them,
And health to all their flesh.

– Proverbs 4:20–22 NKJV

Chapter 1

———— ••«(((•)))»•• ————

Take as Directed

From my own experience, I will share with you how I discovered this wonderful medicine bottle of God. I learned about this great blessing during the early years of World War II. Because I am British, I served in the British Army as a medical orderly (what Americans call a hospital attendant) with the British Medical Services for five-and-a half years during World War II. For the first three years of duty, I was stationed in the deserts of North Africa: first in Egypt, then in Libya, and finally in the Sudan. In the desert the two things that we were exposed to more than anything else were sand and sun. I spent

nearly one entire year in the desert without ever
seeing a paved road. We traveled in sand, we slept
in sand, and very often we had the impression
that we were eating sand. We were exposed to
it day and night. Combined with the sun, it had
a very harmful effect on certain people whose
skin could not protect them adequately from
that kind of exposure. I was one of them. It manifested itself primarily in the condition of my
feet and my hands, where the skin broke down.
I became incapacitated in many ways. The officer
in command of my particular unit struggled to
keep me from being admitted to the hospital
because he knew if I were admitted, he would
lose me in the unit. Consequently, I spent several months hobbling around trying to do my
military duties. However, in the end he had to
let me go into the hospital. I went to three or
four different military medical facilities, and I
was in the hospital for a year. During that time,
I met soldiers there who had been two years in
the Middle East and spent eighteen months in
the hospital with similar conditions.

The doctors gave many elaborate diagno-
ses of my problem. Each name tended to be a

little longer than the previous one. Eventually, my condition was diagnosed simply as chronic eczema. I received the best medical treatment available, but it really did not help me.

I saw many other soldiers with similar conditions who also were not helped. Those with really serious conditions, burns and so on, were usually shipped to South Africa. However, my condition was not considered to be that serious, and my services to the British Army were not so valuable that they were going to waste a passage on a ship to South Africa for me. So I just lay there in bed, day after day, wondering what my future would be. I'll tell you, when you spend an entire year in the hospital, it seems to be an eternity!

Shortly before this time, I had come into a real personal relationship with the Lord, had been born again and received the filling of the Holy Spirit. But I was very ignorant about God's Word then, not having any background in biblical instruction. I had a Bible and really had nowhere else to turn for help but to God and His Word.

In desperation I began to search the Scriptures to see what they could tell me about my physical condition. I didn't have any theories about healing; I just knew I needed it. I had the Bible and plenty of time to read, since there was very little else to do. So I searched through the Bible for something that would show me if I could really trust God for the healing of my body. One day I came across some verses in the book of Proverbs which I learned to call "God's medicine bottle." I am quoting from the King James Version which was the version that I was reading in those days and which is extremely vivid and forceful:

> *My son, give attention to my words;*
> *Incline your ear to my sayings.*
> *Do not let them depart from your eyes;*
> *Keep them in the midst of your heart;*
> *For they are life to those who find them,*
> *And health to all their flesh*
>
> Proverbs 4:20–22 (NKJV)

It was that last phrase, "health to all their flesh," that caught my attention. I understood that "all their flesh" meant the total physical body, which is the way more modern versions translate it. I reasoned with myself, Health! If I have health in my whole body, then I have no room anywhere for sickness. That is what God is promising me.

Then I happened to look in the margin of my Bible and saw that the alternative translation for the word health was the word medicine. That seemed to be even more appropriate for my condition. God was promising me something that would be medicine which would bring health to all my flesh. I thought to myself, That's precisely what I need. So I went back and read those words over and over again. I saw that, in essence, God's offer was being made to me through His Word.

Verse 20 says: "give attention to my words; incline your ear to my sayings." Then verse 22 says: "For they [that's God's words and God's sayings] are life to those who find them, and health to all their flesh." So, somehow life and health are in the words and the sayings of God. I didn't know how that could be, but I knew God was promising it.

When I saw the phrase, "those who find them," I realized this process was more than just reading the Bible. It was reading the Bible in such a way as to find out how to receive what God was offering.

All the medical attention that was available in those conditions had not helped me. So I made a decision, a very naive decision in a way. I decided I was going to take God's Word as my medicine. That was a very crucial point in my life in many ways. When I made that decision, the Lord Himself spoke to me. Not audibly, but nevertheless very clearly, I heard Him say, "When the doctor gives a person medicine, the directions for taking it are on the bottle." Then He instructed, "This is My medicine I'm giving you. The directions are on the bottle. You better study them."

God reminded me that a doctor doesn't promise any benefit from the medicine he recommends unless it is taken according to the directions. Being a medical orderly, I was very aware of that.

I then decided to study the directions on the bottle. Very quickly I saw that there were four specific instructions for taking God's Word as medicine for the physical body. These are His directions:

1. Give attention to My words.
2. Incline incline your ear to My sayings.
3. Do not let them depart from your eyes.
4. Keep them in the midst of your heart.

I realized that if I were going to receive the benefits I needed from the medicine, I had to comply with these four guidelines.

I cannot go in detail into all that followed, but I began to bow my head over the Bible three times every day after meals, because that is how people normally take medicine. I said, "God, You have said that these words of Yours will be medicine to all my flesh, and I'm taking them as my medicine now, in the name of Jesus." Within a few months, God's medicine, taken that way, achieved the result God promised. I was totally healthy in every area of my body.

A good many years ago, I recorded this experience on a tape. Just recently in London, England, I met a young man from Pakistan who told me that he'd become a Christian and that had suffered for more than twenty years from eczema. One day he heard my tape and decided to do what I had done. In his case, he was completely healed within two or three days. So that is an up-to-date testimony that the medicine still does what it claims to do.

Chapter 2

Pay Close Attention

I now want to share with you the lessons I learned about the directions that are on God's medicine bottle and how to apply them. The first of these four instructions is, "give attention to my words." We need to understand that when God speaks to us, He requires our undivided attention. If Almighty God is willing to speak to us at all, surely any sense of propriety would indicate that we need to listen to God with our full and respectful attention. Sadly, that's not really the attitude of many people today. Because of the tremendous proliferation of the media – radio, television, and so on – and because of various different factors in our contemporary culture, we have almost cultivated the practice of listening to two different things at one time. We suffer from a disease which could be called "divided attention." I'm amazed when I go into a home and see teenagers doing their homework while watching television at the same time. They're not giving full attention to either one or the other.

In many places now, we have what is called background music. We carry on a conversation, but at the same time, with one ear we're listening to the music in the background. I have to say that for me, personally, this is intensely frustrating. I am the kind of person who desires to concentrate on something without dissipating my attention. I think that is a characteristic God has conditioned in me which I am not willing to relinquish. If I am having a conversation, I want to listen to the person who is talking. If I am listening to music, then I want to listen to the music. I love music. When I listen to it, I listen to it with my full attention.

But you see, all through the Bible, the primary key to healing from God is hearing. Let me say that simply: the key to biblical healing is hearing. It's what we listen to and how we listen that is so essential. Jesus said to His disciples, "Take heed what you hear" (Mark 4:24 NKJV). He also said, "Take heed how you hear" (Luke 8:18 NKJV). We have to put the two together. It is what we listen to and how we listen to it.

Another passage which relates to healing is found in the Old Testament and brings out the same emphasis. In Exodus, the Lord told Israel, through Moses:

> *"If you will diligently heed the voice of the LORD your God and do what is right in His sight, give ear to His commandments and keep all His statutes, I will put none of the diseases upon you which I have brought upon the Egyptians. For I am the LORD who heals you."*
>
> Exodus 15:26 (NKJV)

Notice that final statement. That goes right along with the medicine bottle instructions: "I provide the medicine, and I am your physician." In modern Hebrew that is exactly how that word would be translated: "I am the Lord, your doctor." God says to His people, "I'm willing to be your doctor, the doctor of your physical body.

However, there are conditions. He begins with an "if."

The first condition, the basic one, is: "If you will diligently heed the voice of the LORD your God." You see, what we listen to is very important. The Hebrew word that is translated "diligently heed," is a repetition of the verb "to listen." It goes something like this: "If you will 'listen, listeningly' to the voice of the LORD your God." The complete emphasis is on listening.

When I was seeking healing for myself I came across this verse in conjunction with Proverbs 4:20–22. I asked myself, What does it mean to 'listen, listeningly'?

God gave me an answer to my question. He said, "You've got two ears, a right ear and a left one; 'to listen, listeningly' means to listen to Me with both ears, with your right ear and with your left. Don't listen to Me with your right ear and something else with your left because the result of that will be confusion."

The emphasis is on attending to God, listening to Him, giving God your undivided attention. That is the primary instruction on God's medicine bottle. It matters what we hear and how we hear. This is not only the key to being healed, it is also the key to receiving faith. Of course, they go very closely together. It is faith that enables us to receive the healing that God has provided and to benefit from the medicine.

One of my favorite Scriptures, which was also made real to me during this long period in the hospital, is the following:

> *So then faith comes by hearing, and hearing by the word of God.*   Romans 10:17 (NKJV)

Lying there in that hospital bed, I was continually saying to myself: I know if I had faith, God would heal me." But then I would say immediately after that: But then, I don't have any faith." When I repeatedly told myself that I didn't have faith, I found myself in what John Bunyan described in Pilgrim's Progress as the "Slough of Despond" – a dark, lonely valley of despair.

One day, as I was reading my Bible, my eyes fell on Romans 10:17: "So then faith comes by hearing, and hearing by the word of God." There were two words that leaped out from the page at me: faith comes. In other words, you don't need to despair. Maybe you don't have faith, but faith comes. If you don't have it, you can get it.

Of course, I looked to see how faith comes. The Word says: "Faith comes by hearing and hearing by the word of God." Again, just as in Proverbs 4:20–22, I was directed right back to the Word of God. As I began to analyze that verse, I saw that we start with the Word of God. That's the beginning. We listen to the Word of God carefully, and, out of that listening, there comes what the Bible calls "hearing," the ability to hear God. Then out of hearing, faith develops.

It is the Word of God which, when we first attend to it, produces hearing. As we continue hearing, or being focused on God's voice, faith develops out of that hearing. In a sense, everything depends on how we approach the Word of God. Do we approach it with undivided attention? Do we listen with both ears? Are we focused on the Word of God? Do we get into a condition, both spiritually and mentally, which the Bible calls hearing, where we are truly able to hear what God is saying to us?

I'm sure many people read the Bible but never hear God. They don't hear God because their minds are occupied with other things. They are wondering how they are going to pay the rent, or what the weather is going to be like, or they are concerned with the political situation. There are other forces at work in their minds. Consequently, they never develop the ability to hear God.

We have to develop hearing, and out of hearing faith develops. God's Word itself and the right attitude toward God's Word produce hearing. When we are able to hear, then faith comes. We are always directed back to the Word of God and how we are to receive it.

Thus, the first instruction on God's medicine bottle is, "Give attention to my words."

Chapter 3

———◆◉◆———

Bend Your Ear

Now I'm going to explain the second of the instructions God has given for taking His medicine: "incline your ear."

The word *incline* is slightly old English, so we need to make sure that we understand precisely what it means. "To incline" is to bend down, and "an incline" is a hill that slopes. So, "inclining your ear" is bending your ear down.

A fact of the human body is that you cannot bend your ear without bending your head down. In inclining your ear, you are actually inclining your head. What does that express? It is an attitude indicating humility and teachability. I will illustrate it from experience.

As I was studying the Bible in the hospital, seeking desperately for the answer to my problem, I read many promises of healing, blessing and prosperity. But my attitude was conditioned by my background, which is probably true of all of us.

My background was in a segment of the Christian church where Christianity was not associated with being happy – in fact, very much the opposite. I had early in life formed the conclusion that if I were going to be a Christian, I would have to be prepared to be miserable. I had also decided pretty early that I was not prepared to be miserable and, therefore, I wasn't going to be a Christian. It was only a sovereign intervention of God in my life that changed me, but I still carried a lot of these old concepts with me.

When I found these repeated promises in the Bible of healing, health, strength, long life, prosperity and abundance, I kept shaking my head – not inclining my head, but shaking my head – and saying: "This couldn't be! That's too good to be true! I can't believe that religion would be like that!" I was reacting this way to one of these statements in Psalms where it says:

"[God] Who forgives all your iniquities, Who heals all your diseases ... so that your youth is renewed like the eagle's." (Psalm 103:3, 5). I told myself: You know, that's impossible. God couldn't be like that. I mean, we know we have to anticipate misery being Christians.

As I was responding like that inwardly, God spoke to me so clearly, not audibly, but just as clearly as someone was actually speaking. He said: "Now tell Me, who is the pupil and who is the teacher?" I thought it over for a moment and I replied: "Lord, You're the teacher and I'm the pupil." Then He responded: "Well, would you mind letting Me teach you?"

I saw then that I was not letting God teach me at all. I had my own preconceptions. If He said something different in His Word, I really was not capable of hearing it because my mind was blocked by these set ideas. God in essence was saying: "Incline your ear, give up your prejudices, bend that stiff neck of yours, and let Me tell you how good I am and how wonderful is the provision I've made for you. Don't measure Me by human standards because I'm God. I'm almighty and gracious, a faithful and merciful God."

This brings out a very important principle about God's Word. God's Word works in us only insofar as we receive it. If we don't receive it, it doesn't do us any good. In a very powerful passage, James said when he was speaking about God:

> *Of His own will He brought us forth by the word of truth,* [Notice, our becoming Christians is due to the Word. God begat us with the word of truth.] *that we might be a kind of firstfruits of His creatures.*
>
> *So then, my beloved brethren, let every man be swift to hear, slow to speak, slow to wrath;* [Note that: a wise man is swift to hear, but slow to speak.]
>
> *Therefore lay aside all filthiness and [b]overflow of wickedness, and receive with meekness the implanted word, which is able to save your souls.*
> James 1:18–19, 21 (NKJV)

God's Word can save you, it can heal you, and it can bless you in innumerable ways, but only if you receive it with meekness. One of the things that we have to lay aside is naughtiness.

We usually associate naughtiness with children. What is a naughty child? One of the marks of a naughty child is answering back when he is taught or reproved. God says: "Don't answer Me back. When I tell you something, don't argue with Me. Don't tell Me you think it can't be true or that it's impossible or that I couldn't mean that. Let Me teach you." That is the essence of the inclined ear. It means that we come to God and we say, "God, You're the teacher; I'm the pupil. I'm willing to let You teach me. I bow down my ear and I listen."

In this matter of inclining the ear, we have to come face to face with the fact that most of us have mental barriers when we begin to read the Bible. They are due, in many cases, to our backgrounds. Many of us have had some kind of denominational affiliation in the past. We may still be active members of some particular denomination. I am not opposed to denominations, but I want to suggest to you that every denomination has its weak points and its strong points. It has areas in which it has been faithful to the truth, and it has areas in which it has not been faithful to the truth. If we measure God from our own denominational background, if we judge the Scriptures by what some church or some denomination teaches, we will exclude from our minds much of the truth that God wants us to receive and which can bless and help us.

For instance, some churches teach that the age of miracles is past. I have never been able to find any basis for that statement in Scripture. I can think of dozens of Scriptures which indicate the exact opposite. But if you approach it with the attitude that the age of miracles is past, then when God promises you a miracle, you probably can't hear Him or receive it.

Some Christian groups suggest that in order to be holy, you have to be poor. Being anything but poor is considered in some way almost sinful. Well, if it is God's purpose to bless you with material prosperity in order for you to help build His kingdom, as He states many times in Scripture, it can be His purpose. But if you have the attitude that you must be poor, you won't be able to receive the blessing of prosperity which God is offering you on the basis of Scripture. There is a Scripture which I think most of us really need to take to heart.

Beloved, I pray that you may prosper in all things and be in health, just as your soul prospers.   3 John 2 (NKJV)

I remember when I started to read that verse, it knocked me over. My old prejudices and preconceptions rose up. I thought: That's impossible. It can't mean what it says." But, you see, God said, "Incline your ear. Don't come at Me with your arguments, your prejudices, your preconceptions. Bend that stiff neck of yours and let Me teach you." That is an essential requirement for receiving healing through the Word of God. By laying down our preconceptions and prejudices, bending our stiff necks and opening our ears, we become able to listen carefully to what God says and not reject it because it doesn't agree with something we thought God ought to have said.

God is a lot bigger than any denomination. He is a lot bigger than our understanding. He is a lot bigger than all of our prejudices. Don't make God so small that He can't help you. Incline your ear and let Him tell you how much He is willing to do for you.

Chapter 4

————— ⦿ —————

Don't Let Them Out of Your Sight

I have dealt with the first two directions on God's medicine bottle: "Give attention to my words" and "Incline thine ear." So logically, I am moving on to the third instruction: "Do not let them depart from your eyes." The word "them" refers to God's words and God's sayings.

The key thought in this directive could be summed up in the word *focus*. One of the marvelous things about human eyes, which is not true of certain other animals or creatures, is that we have two eyes, but by focusing we can form one image. Of course, that is when our eyesight is healthy and operating the way God intended. In the natural with good eyesight, incorrect focus produces blurred vision. I believe that is the problem with many people in the spiritual realm. They haven't yet learned to focus their spiritual eyesight, so their vision of spiritual things is blurred.

I think most people have the impression that the spiritual world is kind of misty, half-real, vague, unformed. I know that was my impression of religion before I came to know the Lord in a personal way. I thought of religion as a kind of mist that hung around in old church buildings. I formulated that if I were very good, then perhaps the mist would settle on my head, but it never did. So after a while I just decided that I was not interested in that, and I turned elsewhere to philosophy. But the fact remains that unless we can focus our spiritual eyes, we will always have a blurred vision of spiritual reality. Look at the words of Jesus in dealing with spiritual vision:

> *The light of the body is the eye: therefore when thine eye is single, thy whole body also is full of light; but when thine eye is evil, thy body also is full of darkness.*
>
> (Luke 11:34 KJV)

Here Jesus is speaking about something that affects the whole body. Instantly, it reminds me of the statement in Proverbs 4 about God's words being health to our whole body. But here Jesus is dealing with the way we use our eyes. "When thine eye is single" – I think that means, first and foremost, that we form a single image or focus. We are not looking in different directions with our two eyes, but they are focused to make one image. Then Jesus says the result will be manifested in the whole body: "Thy whole body is full of light."

I believe a body that is full of light does not have room for sickness. I believe light and darkness are mutually exclusive. Sickness is from darkness. Health is from light:

> *But to you who fear My name the Sun of Righteousness shall arise with healing in His wings.*
> Malachi 4:2 (NKJV)

The sun, in the natural, is the source of light. The two products of light, when the sun arises, are righteousness and healing. They are the works of light. The opposite are the works of darkness. The opposite of righteousness is sin;

the opposite of healing is sickness. They are works of darkness, but righteousness and healing are works of light. Jesus is saying: "If your eye is singly focused, your whole body will be filled with light, with righteousness, with health." It all depends on having a single eye. The Greek word that has been translated as *single* is a word that has various meanings, which I rather carefully checked in two Greek lexicons before I finished preparing this. One of the main meanings is "simple" or "sincere," which I think probably brings out the point. If your eye is simple or sincere, if you just see things the way they are written, then you are not too clever or too philosophical. You do not know too many different ways of explaining the text away: you just take it as meaning what it says.

I previously explained that the second direction, "incline your ear," means bow down your stiff neck, be willing to hear. There are certain normal barriers, and I have described two of them as prejudice and preconception. We think we already know what God ought to have said, so we are not willing to listen.

This third direction speaks about simplicity

or sincerity. I would suggest that the barriers to simplicity and sincerity are rationalization and sophistication. I become wary when I hear preachers quoting too many worldly experts, especially if they are trying to authenticate the Bible. I do not believe that the Bible needs to be authenticated by worldly experts. In the end, that does not build people's faith.

Sooner or later, as I have said earlier, faith comes by hearing the Word of God, and anything that distracts our attention too long from God's Word is not ultimately going to build our faith. We have to read the Bible with that single eye of simplicity and sincerity which says: "This is what God says, this is what He means, and I believe it the way it is written."

I think back to my own experience in the hospital. There I was, a professor of philosophy with a knowledge of Latin and Greek, able to quote many long and learned books. As sick as I was, I was offered, through God's Word a very simple, unsophisticated way of getting healed: taking God's Word as my medicine. Now, to a philosophic mind, that is pure nonsense! It is just ridiculous! You dismiss it. But, you see, I was sick, and philosophy hadn't healed me. So I was really faced with two clear alternatives: I could be clever and stay sick, or I could be simple and get healed.

One thing I have always been glad about ever since – I became simple enough to get healed.

That brings out this point: if your eye is simple, if you are sincere, if you are not too profound, if you do not know too many arguments, if you cannot quote all the theologians, then you have a much better chance to reach God. I am sorry to say it, but experience over many years has convinced me of that. Theology normally does not help people's faith.

Let me quote two passages from the writings of Paul to conclude this thought. Note that we are talking about a kind of simplicity which, in the eyes of the world, is foolish. Paul wrote on this subject:

> *Because the foolishness of God is wiser than men, and the weakness of God is stronger than men.*
> 1 Corinthians 1:25 (NKJV)

He is speaking primarily about the cross. The cross was the weakest and most foolish thing that you could conceive of in the culture of that time, but out of the weakness of the cross comes the almightiness of God. Out of the foolishness of the cross comes the unsearchable wisdom of God. So we have to go to something very weak and very foolish to receive God's wisdom and God's strength.

A little further on, in 1 Corinthians, Paul says something very interesting. Because I realize that he was speaking to people with a philosophic background just like I acquired through my studies, I can appreciate it so well.

> *Let no one deceive himself. If anyone among you seems to be wise in this age, let him become a fool that he may become wise.*
>
> 1 Corinthians 3:18 (NKJV)

You see, between us and God's wisdom is a valley, a place of humility. We have to lay aside worldly wisdom. We have to become fools in the eyes of the world in order that we may really enter into God's wisdom.

At that point, I was confronted with an alternative. I could go on being wise in the world and stay sick, or I could do something that was foolish in the eyes of the world and get healed. I actually have to say, I was much wiser to be foolish and get healed than I would have been to be clever and stay sick. That may sound confusing, but it is exactly what Paul is saying: "If you are wise in this world, you need to become a fool in order that you may be wise, because God's foolishness is much wiser than man's."

The application is: "Don't let them depart from your eyes." Have a single, simple eye. Read the Bible the way it was written, and take it as meaning what it says.

Chapter 5

―――●●●―――

Keep Them in Your Heart

We have already looked at the first three directions concerning how to receive God's medicine. Now we are coming to the fourth and final instruction about His words and sayings: "Keep them in the midst of your heart."

This directive is very real to me for two reasons. The first is based on my own experience of being healed through this passage. The second reason is that for five years I was principal of a college in East Africa which trained African teachers for African schools. Therefore, of course, I had to familiarize myself with some of the principles of teaching. One of the simple principles that we used to try to inculcate knowledge into our students was the principle of what we call the "ear gate" and the "eye gate." When you want to engage a child's total attention, you need to engage every available gate. It is not enough for the child just to hear; the child also needs to see. In fact, we also taught them that a child not merely needs to hear and see, but must also become practically involved: hear, see, and do. It blesses me to see that, in this passage in Proverbs, God anticipated the psychology of modern education theory by about 3,000 years. He said, "Incline your ear; let them not depart from your eyes, then they will get into your heart." You see, the purpose of going through the ear gate and the eye gate is to reach that vital, central area of human personality which the Bible calls the heart. When their hearts are reached, students will do what they promise. But if their hearts are not touched, positive results will not be produced.

In order to be effective, some kinds of medicine which you take must be released into the bloodstream. You can take the medicine, but if it does not get to the bloodstream, it is not going to do what it is supposed to do. Well, God's medicine is only effective when it is released in the heart. The previous three directions are all concerned with the medicine getting where it will do what is promised, which is the heart. Then it says: "Keep them in the midst of your heart."

We need to look on to the very next verse of Proverbs which is one of the most profound verses in the Bible:

> *Keep your heart with all diligence, for out of it spring the issues of life.*
>
> Proverbs 4:23 (NKJV)

How profound that is: "Out of [the heart] spring the issues of life."

My mind goes back again to East Africa. One of my students wrote this verse in her own vernacular language which was called Lorlagoli. I knew just enough to be able to read what she had written on the dormitory wall. It said, "Guard your heart with all of your strength; for all the things in life come out of it." It is so simple, more simple in a sense than the New King James Version.

The conviction never left me that all the things in life do come out of your heart.

In other words, what you have in your heart will determine all that you experience in your life. If you have the right thing in your heart, your life will go right. If you have the wrong thing in your heart, your life will go wrong.

However, it is what is in your heart that determines the course of your life. So God says: "If My medicine and My words and My sayings are going to do what I have promised, they must get into your heart, and you must keep them there. 'Keep them in the midst of your heart' – not just on the periphery of your heart, but in the middle. Keep them in the central place of your whole life and personality. They are going to affect the whole way that you live."

To conclude this teaching about God's Word being our medicine, I would like to turn to a parallel statement in the New Testament. Hebrews 4:12 speaks about the nature of God's Word and how it acts within us. In order to make it vivid, I am going to quote two different translations so we can pick out certain differences between the versions. First is the King James Version:

For the word of God is quick, and powerful, and sharper than any two-edged sword, pierc-

ing even to the dividing asunder of soul and
spirit, and of the joints and marrow, and is a
discerner of the thoughts and intents of the heart.

Hebrews 4:12 (KJV)

The New American Standard reads:

For the word of God is living and active and
sharper than any two-edged sword, and pierc-
ing as far as the division of soul and spirit, of
both joints and marrow, and able to judge the
thoughts and intentions of the heart.

Hebrews 4:12 (NAS)

If I were to choose one word that sums this
up, I think it would be the word *penetrating*.
God's Word penetrates. In fact, it penetrates
where nothing else can penetrate. We are used to
the concept of the surgeon's knife with its sharp,
pointed blade that can penetrate so delicately
into human tissue. But the Word of God penetrates into another realm. It divides between
soul and spirit, the very innermost areas of our
personality. Things within ourselves that we
cannot fully understand about ourselves, the
Word of God reveals to us. It separates between
joint and marrow. It touches the spiritual area of

us, and it touches the physical area. There is no area of our lives that is out of its reach.

If you have a disease of the marrow or a disease of the joints, this Scripture says that maybe there's no human medicine or human instrument that can deal with it, but the Word of God can get there. If you have inner personality problems for which the psychiatrist does not have a solution, the Word of God will get there. God's Word penetrates.

What is important is that we take God's Word the way He Himself requires that we take it. We must take it with our undivided attention and with a humble, teachable attitude. We must lay down our barriers of prejudice and preconception and look at it with a single, sincere, wholehearted eye. We do not want to quibble; we do not want to theorize too much. We must take it as meaning what it says. We must lay down the barriers of rationalization and sophistication, and then we can let it enter and do its work.

Closing Prayer

Heavenly Father,

I thank you for those who have been reading this book who have spiritual and physical needs that can only be solved by the Word of God. I pray that this word will enter in and do what is necessary in them: create faith, bring healing, bring deliverance, bring peace and joy and harmony. All of this I pray in the name of Jesus.

Amen.

About the Author

————— ◉ —————

Derek Prince (1915–2003) was born in India of British parents. Educated as a scholar of Greek and Latin at Eton College and Cambridge University, England, he held a Fellowship in Ancient and Modern Philosophy at King's College. He also studied several modern languages, including Hebrew and Aramaic, at Cambridge University and the Hebrew University in Jerusalem.

While serving with the British army in World War II, he began to study the Bible and experienced a life-changing encounter with Jesus Christ. Out of this encounter he formed two conclusions: first, that Jesus Christ is alive; second, that the Bible is a true, relevant, up-to-date book. These conclusions altered the whole course of his life, which he then devoted to studying and teaching the Bible.

Derek's main gift of explaining the Bible and its teaching in a clear and simple way has helped build a foundation of faith in millions of lives. His non-denominational, non-sectarian approach has made his teaching equally relevant and helpful to people from all racial and religious backgrounds.

He is the author of over 50 books, 600 audio and 100 video teachings, many of which have been translated and published in more than 100 languages. His daily radio broadcast is translated into Arabic, Chinese (Amoy, Cantonese, Mandarin, Shanghainese, Swatow), Croatian, German, Malagasy, Mongolian, Russian, Samoan, Spanish and Tongan. The radio program continues to touch lives around the world.

Derek Prince Ministries persists in reaching out to believers in over 140 countries with Derek's teachings, fulfilling the mandate to keep on "until Jesus returns." This is effected through the outreaches of more than 45 Derek Prince offices around the world, including primary work in Australia, Canada, China, France, Germany, the Netherlands, New Zealand, Norway, Russia, South Africa, Switzerland, the United Kingdom and the United States. For current information about these and other worldwide locations, visit www.derekprince.com.

FROM BITTERNESS TO JOY

In this book Derek Prince teaches on an issue that has touched all our lives in one way or another – bitter disappointment. How we deal with bitterness either will make us or break us. Often man's disappointments are God's appointments – but we can only discover His purposes in them as we respond in faith. Learn the right way to handle hard times!

ISBN: 978-1-78263-581-9
Paperback: £4.99

THE THREE MOST POWERFUL WORDS:
I FORGIVE YOU

Do you know the three most power words? According to Derek Prince, they are, 'I forgive you.'

The Bible clearly points out, that as long as you resist forgiving others, you allow the enemy legal access into your life. This can cause you damage and can even provoke God's anger. This book can help you to say, 'I forgive you', and mean it. It can enable you to see how God can empower your prayers, tear down hindrances to healing and open the pathway to receiving His blessings into your life.

978-1-78263-424-9
Paperback: £4.99

www.dpmuk.org/shop

WHAT DID YOU SAY?

Words shape your destiny! The Bible declares that death and life are found in the power of the tongue. Every Christian knows it is imperative to keep the tongue under control but, sooner or later, finds that he cannot do so himself.

Derek Prince provides clear, biblical steps to discipline the tongue, the steps needed for healing, the importance of confession, and more so that your words will be spoken for God's glory and your blessing!

978-1-78263-587-1
Paperback: £5.99

DPM Offices Worldwide

DPM – Asia/Pacific
38 Hawdon Street
Sydenham
Christchurch 8023
New Zealand
T: + 64 3 366 4443
E: admin@dpm.co.nz
W: www.dpm.co.nz and www.derekprince.in

DPM – Australia
15 Park Road
Seven Hills
New South Wales 2147
Australia
T: +61 2 9838 7778
E: enquiries@au.derekprince.com
W: www.derekprince.com.au

DPM – Canada
P.O. Box 8354 Halifax
Nova Scotia B3K 5M1
Canada
T: + 1 902 443 9577
E: enquiries.dpm@eastlink.ca
W: www.derekprince.org

DPM – France
B.P. 31, Route d'Oupia
34210 Olonzac
France
T: + 33 468 913872
E: info@derekprince.fr
W: www.derekprince.fr

DPM – Germany
Söldenhofstr. 10
83308 Trostberg
Germany
T: + 49 8621 64146
E: ibl@ibl-dpm.net
W: www.ibl-dpm.net

DPM – Netherlands

Nijverheidsweg 12
7005 BJ Doetinchem
Netherlands
T: +31 251–255044
E: info@derekprince.nl
W: www.derekprince.nl

DPM – Norway

P.O. Box 129
Lodderfjord
N-5881 Bergen
Norway
T: +47 928 39855
E: sverre@derekprince.no
W: www.derekprince.no

Derek Prince Publications Pte. Ltd.

P.O. Box 2046
Robinson Road Post Office
Singapore 904046
T: + 65 6392 1812
E: dpmchina@singnet.com.sg
W: www.dpmchina.org (English)
   www.ygmweb.org (Chinese)

DPM – South Africa
P.O. Box 33367
Glenstantia
0010 Pretoria
South Africa
T: +27 12 348 9537
E: enquiries@derekprince.co.za
W: www.derekprince.co.za

DPM – Switzerland
Alpenblick 8
CH-8934 Knonau
Switzerland
T: + 41 44 768 25 06
E: dpm-ch@ibl-dpm.net
W: www.ibl-dpm.net

DPM – UK
PO Box 393
Hitchin SG5 9EU
United Kingdom
T: + 44 1462 492100
E: enquiries@dpmuk.org
W: www.dpmuk.org

DPM – USA

P.O. Box 19501

Charlotte NC 28219

USA

T: + 1 704 357 3556

E: ContactUs@derekprince.org

W: www.derekprince.org

Milton Keynes UK
Ingram Content Group UK Ltd.
UKHW022147280923
429540UK00008B/68